How to Bully-Proof Your Child -
A Parents' Guide

First published in 2013 by CreateBooks New Zealand

National Library of New Zealand Cataloguing-in-Publication Data

Title:	How to Bully-Proof Your Child
Author:	Ann Neville
Publisher:	CreateBooks
Address:	www.createbooks.co.nz
	info@createbooks.co.nz
Format:	Paperback
Publication Date:	2013
ISBN:	978-0-473-24984-7

Cover and inside illustrations by Scott Pearson

Visual Evolution: www.visualevolution.co.nz

How to Bully-Proof Your Child - A Parents' Guide

by Ann Neville

How to Bully-Proof Your Child - A Parents' Guide

This book addresses the following issues:

1. What bullying is.
2. What bullying is NOT!
3. Who gets targeted and why.
4. How to tell if your child is being bullied.
5. Who can help and which authorities should be contacted in certain circumstances.
6. What children themselves can do.
7. What parents can do.
8. What witnesses can do.
9. The bullies themselves.
10. The critical role of parents/care givers.

What is bullying?

Bullying is one of the major issues facing many children, parents, educators and the community at large. Although bullying has always occurred, it seems that this behaviour has been underestimated in both its extent and severity. The long-term effects bullying has on the victim and the perpetrator have also been underrated.

Children get bullied for a variety of reasons including:

- ethnicity
- resistance to pressure to behave in a certain way
- physical differences
- high achievement/low achievement
- being new
- sexual orientation
- socio-economic background
- religious beliefs

Preferred victims are often passive, hesitant and socially awkward.

Bullying may be either direct or indirect harassment, a minor nuisance or more severe abuse. The abuse may be physical or verbal and involve extortion and exclusion. It may involve criminal acts such as sexual harassment, racial abuse, deprivation of human rights and cyber bullying. The most common form is repeated verbal harassment.

What bullying is NOT!

Isolated incidents are **NOT** bullying e.g.

- single episodes of social rejection or dislike
- single-episodes of nastiness or spite
- isolated acts of aggression or intimidation
- mutual arguments and disagreements

Children need to understand that conflict is a normal part of everyday life and need to be given the skills to deal with isolated incidents. While recognising that isolated incidents are **NOT** classified as bullying, they do still need to be addressed.

However, if the acts are repeated and/or increase in severity it's time to bring in the **BULLYBUSTING** strategies.

The good news?

There are many children who are NOT bullied despite appearing to be exactly the same type of child as those who are.

What makes the difference?

This is where **YOU**, the parent/care giver, can play a significant role.

Who gets targeted and why?

Any child can be bullied just by being in the wrong place at the wrong time. Sometimes the exact things that can make a child accepted in one group can make him/her a victim of bullying in another. However, in most cases, the bully picks on children who appear 'easy' targets.

Bullies set their sights on:

- Anyone who is different – their looks, weight, accent, clothing or interests. Disabilities make some children an easy target,
- Those who are small or young – and not so able to defend themselves,
- Those who will react quickly – popular targets are children who get upset or cry easily
- Anyone who is socially anxious or struggles with shyness,
- Individuals who have low self-esteem or personal power,
- Those who are 'over' confident.

Often bullies are repeating the same patterns of adult behaviours they see around them or are subjected to themselves.

Gender differences in bullying: boys tend to engage in more physical bullying, and girls in social or relational bullying. However, this is changing and some girls are becoming more physically aggressive.

Is your child being bullied?

If your child is being bullied, he/she will feel scared, lonely and hopeless. You may find it difficult to get them to admit it to you. They may feel ashamed and believe that they have brought the bullying on themselves. They may think that it's 'dobbing' to tell, or they may have been threatened with worse treatment if they tell.

If your child is the victim of bullying, he/she may:

- Try to avoid school by faking illness, or even run away from school
- Want to change his/her route to school, or ask you to take them to school
- Feel excluded or ignored by other children
- Become tearful at the thought of going to school
- Let his/her school work suffer because of their stress levels
- Resist talking to you about his/her day at school
- Get angry when you talk about what's going on in his/her life
- Have unexplained injuries
- Feel too anxious to eat or begin to over-eat
- Lose self-confidence
- Have nightmares
- Begin wetting the bed

Who can help and which authorities should be contacted in certain circumstances?

ALL abuse (and that is what bullying is!) should be addressed but it depends on the type and severity of abuse as to how.

If at all possible the first line of action should, with your help, be your child him/herself! While your child may not be able to completely stop people from saying bad things, he/she does have control over how he/she responds to it.

School - All schools are required to have an anti-bullying policy. Your child has a right to feel safe at school. So what should you do if your child is being bullied at school? This advice comes from www.healthpages.co.nz

- Contact the school to set up a meeting with your child's teacher and any other relevant school staff to discuss what is going on and to seek a way to resolve the bullying.
- Stay calm during the meeting, even though you may feel angry or upset about what is happening to your child.
- Be specific about how your child is being bullied
- Do not place blame on the teacher – they may have no idea that the bullying is going on.

- Discuss what the school's policy is on bullying and whether there is any support available for your child – counselling, mediation, etc.
- Discuss the plan of action that the school will take to stop the bullying.
- Set up another meeting in two week's time to discuss progress.

Doctor – your GP will have suggestions as to what to do and who can help.

Police

Human Rights Commission – According to The Commission (www.hrc.co.nz) it can help in two ways:

- Provide advice and links to organisations with specific responsibilities for dealing with complaints about bullying at school.
- Help sort the problem directly, particularly if the bullying or harassment is linked to one of the grounds of discrimination in the Human Rights Act (such as someone's sex, race, sexual orientation or disability).

A list of resources, including online sites and phone lines, is given in the References and Further Reading section of this booklet.

What can you as a parent do?

Confidence seems to be a critical element in not being bullied. BUT BEWARE! High self-esteem often correlates with egotism, self-deception and defensiveness. These traits themselves can lead to children being bullied. So there's more to it than mere confidence.

Perhaps **self-acceptance** is a more useful attribute. After all, no-one is perfect but if we can look at ourselves objectively then we have a choice.

- With things that can be changed we can either choose to put the effort in and make those changes. Or we choose to accept the status quo (and the consequences).
- With things that *cannot* be changed there is no choice – we have to 'bite the bullet', accept it and concentrate on the positives.

Through objective self-acceptance we are able to rely on our own judgement of the way things are. This enables us to be less emotionally influenced by the opinions of others e.g. bullies.

Your role as a parent/care giver is critical in guiding your child in his/her journey to positive self-acceptance.

What else can parents do?

Children who are the frequent victims of bullies often grow up to be bullied adults. Take steps to break the cycle now and guarantee that your child will be bullied no more.

The key to helping children is in providing them with strategies to deal with bullying on an everyday basis and also help restore their self-esteem and regain a sense of dignity.

- Teach your child that while they may not be able to completely stop what is happening to them, they do have total control over how they react to it. This gives them power. Suggestions as to how to act/react follow.

- Encourage your child to stay with groups of friends. Bullies generally pass over victims that have even one or two friends with them.

- Encourage your child to voice his/her objections to bullying behaviour. Bullies prefer victims who suffer in silence. Practice role-playing until your child can firmly tell someone to stop picking on him. (For notes on role-playing see Appendix I.)

- Arm your child with funny comebacks. An audience is important to a bully, so if your child can make a clever (though not mean-spirited) retort, often the audience will begin to side with the victim, thus undermining the bully's power.

- Teach your child to carry him/herself with confidence. Actions can be learned, even without the internal confidence to back them up. Bullies choose their victims based on an *appearance* of weakness, so teach your child to stand up straight and look people in the eye - especially when confronted.

- Get self-defence training for your child. Although a violent response to a bully is not acceptable nor productive, self-defence classes can make a child feel more confident and therefore become less of a target.

- It may be tempting to tell a child to fight back. After all, you're angry that your child is suffering and maybe you were told to 'stand up for yourself' when you were young. And you may worry that your child will continue to suffer at the hands of the bully. But it's important to advise children not to respond to bullying by fighting or bullying back. That can quickly escalate into further violence, trouble, and someone getting injured. Instead, it's best to walk away from the situation, hang out with others, and tell an adult.

- Of course, if it is absolutely impossible to avoid a physical fight, that self-defense course will come in handy! But it must only be used in self-defense.

Stress that your child should:

NEVER be disrespectful to ANYONE: We don't have to agree with everyone or even like everyone. But we do need to respond respectfully. Discuss ways to respond in any given situation. For instance, if a bully says something unkind, your child could respond, 'Hmmm, that's an interesting point of view. I'll think about it.' And then walk off.

It may be tempting to say, 'Hmm I'd like to agree with you... but then we'd both be wrong.' Not a good idea because that is being as disrespectful as the bully!

What other responses can you and your child come up with? Make a list – remember that some children are visual learners and so will remember things that are written down more easily than if they just hear them.

Trust their own assessment of themselves: When someone says something unkind to them, encourage your child to look at the comment objectively. If the criticism is valid, the child can do something about it. If it is not, which is generally the case, the child can dismiss it and make a decision to not feel bad/intimidated about it.

Possible response? 'Thanks for thinking about me but I'm happy with the way I am.'

Not give the bully a chance. Get your child to, as much as possible, avoid the bully. They can't go into hiding or skip class, of course. But if they can take a safer route to school and avoid the bully, great! Check out another route with your child so he/she becomes familiar with it and feels safe. Or suggest they make sure they have someone supportive with them so that they're not alone with the bully (see next tip).

Get a buddy (and be a buddy). Two is better than one if trying to avoid being bullied. Help your child make a plan to walk with a friend or two on the way to school or wherever they might meet the bully. Get them to offer to do the same if a friend is having bully trouble.

What does your child do if they see bullying going on in school - do they tell an adult, stick up for the child being bullied, or tell the bully to stop?

Hold the anger. It's natural to get upset by the bully, but that's what bullies thrive on. It makes them feel powerful. Encourage your child to practice not reacting by crying or looking upset. It takes a lot of practice, but it's a useful skill for keeping off a bully's radar. Sometimes children find it useful to practice 'cool down' strategies such as counting to 10, writing down their angry words, taking deep breaths or walking away. Sometimes the best thing to do is teach children to wear a 'poker face' until they are clear of any danger.

Stand tall and act brave. Acknowledge the fact that when someone is scared of another person, they're probably not feeling their bravest. But sometimes just acting brave is enough to stop a bully. Discuss how a brave person might look and act e.g. Stand tall to send the message: 'Don't mess with me.' Then role play with your child until they feel comfortable with the stance.

Of course, it's easier to feel brave when you feel good about yourself. See the next tip!

Feel good about themselves. Nobody's perfect, but what can your child do to look and feel his/her best? Is there anything they could do to improve their image of themselves? Is there anything YOU could do to improve their self image? (Refer to the section entitled 'How does your behaviour impact on your child.)

Remove the incentive. If the bully is demanding lunch money, start taking a packed lunch. (Hey, but what if the bully demands the packed lunch? Put something disgusting in the sandwiches like... worms! Just kidding.) If the bully is trying to get some particular equipment, don't take it to school.

TELL AN ADULT. Impress on your child that it's not being a tell-tale or nark. In fact, it takes a lot of courage to talk about this kind of thing, and sometimes it takes a while to feel strong enough to talk about it. Make sure your child understands that is okay. Impress on them that, in the end, telling a safe person is the bravest thing a child can do. It can make the child feel really good when he/she takes steps to stay safe and happy and stop the abuse from happening.

They should find someone they trust and tell them what is happening. Teachers, principals and parents can all help to stop bullying. Sometimes bullies stop as soon as a teacher finds out because they're afraid that they will be punished. This is not telling tales - bullying is wrong and it helps if everyone who gets bullied or sees someone being bullied speaks up.

The most important thing is to tell someone. If that person doesn't act, the child needs to tell someone else, or even several people if that's what it takes, until someone does take action to stop the abuse from happening. Children who let adults know that someone is hurting them, even if it's someone they love, might be helping other children as well as themselves.

Discuss with your child who a safe/trustworthy person might be. You? Student advisors? School teacher or counsellor, ...?

How does your behaviour impact on your child?

I'm sure you already know and do this but it's worth revisiting anyway.

As mentioned earlier, bullies are often repeating the same patterns of adult behaviours they see around them. Could this be turned around to help you and your child? What patterns of behaviours do you model in front of your child to help him/her learn how to deal with stressful situations?

Children are like sponges - they absorb everything around them and that is why parents have to be cautious of how they react in certain situations. No parent is perfect and every parent overreacts once a while by yelling, losing their patience, or thinking negatively. Take heart - that's normal! It only becomes a problem when parents act like this consistently.

When the adults in the household consistently overreact or constantly think negatively these behaviours can soon be absorbed by the child. Children need adults to show them how to act and react positively/responsibly/ respectfully. They need adults to model how to carry themselves and how to cope in adverse situations. These constructive lessons help children to find their place in society.

For instance:

- When an adult makes a mistake they should not call themselves stupid and belittle themselves in front of their children. When children see a parent do this, they see that the parent does not respect him/herself. Instead a parent could say, 'Oops, I made a mistake. I'm upset but I will try to fix it.'

- When something goes wrong e.g. spills or breaks occur, parents should not huff and puff, yell or suck on their teeth. Reacting in annoyance and frustration will teach children that mistakes should not be made. (They might even start to accidentally spill and break stuff just to get a reaction out of you).

A positive parent will just pick up the mess and move on, and let the children know it is okay. Don't punish them for it. Instead, if possible have them help you clean up the accident. Working together to clean up a spill or break teaches children that it is okay to make mistakes, and they see their parent acting in a positive manner, one they can adopt themselves.

- When parents encounter rude people or unsatisfactory customer service, parents should not get abusive. When children see this they learn how to be aggressive and hostile rather than how to be tolerant and respectful. They learn that it is only aggressive behavior that can resolve a situation.

Positive parents will speak firmly but respectfully in a non-confrontational manner. This teaches their children to handle situations while still maintaining their own self respect and the respect of others.

- When things do not go as planned, parents should avoid whining, complaining in excess, or slamming doors. Avoid saying, 'I can't do it,' or 'I give up.' This attitude promotes low self-esteem and demotivates both the adult and the child.
- At children's sports events and shows parents should not exhibit extreme competitive behaviour. Cheer your child on by acknowledging the positive things he/she does. Interact with other parents in only positive, respectful ways. Parents who model positive behaviour at events teach their children to be 'good sports', and to value their achievements and improvements.

Remember that children mirror parents
so be careful how you act in your child's presence.

What about cyber bullying?

Cyber bullying is just as devastating for those being targeted as any other form of bullying. What can parents do?

Be cyber savvy

Learn everything you can about information and communication technologies and how your child is using them. Talk to them about the places and sites they go to online and the activities that they are involved in.

Learn how to block access to bullies on your child's mobile, and how to de-friend someone from their face book page, etc.

Encourage communication

Provide an environment in which your child will come to you if anybody says or does something that makes them feel uncomfortable or threatened online or via mobile phone. Stay calm. If you overreact they won't turn to you for help when they need it.

Watch for signs that your child is being bullied online

These could include a reluctance to use the computer or go to school or any of the other behaviours mentioned earlier.

Take action

If the bullying is coming from a student at the same school, meet with school staff and ask for help in resolving the situation. It may even be appropriate to go to the police. New legislation makes it an offence to send messages or post material online that is grossly offensive, indecent, obscene, menacing or knowingly false.

Talk to your child about responsible computer and mobile phone use

Teach them to never post or say anything that they wouldn't want the whole world - including you - to see or read.

Monitor computer use and know your child's log-ins

To keep children safe parents need to have access to their email, private messaging and social networking accounts. It's not invading their privacy when it is used to keep them safe.

What can witnesses do?
DOING NOTHING CONDONES THE BEHAVIOUR.

Determining what to do depends on the level of risk in a particular bullying situation. Encourage your child to make a safe choice. Discuss different levels of risk in choosing an action before intervening. Is it safe to step between the bully and the victim and say, '**STOP'?** If not, what other options are there?

Could they:

- Report to an adult
- Encourage the peer group to take a stand
- Take an individual stand
- Be friendly toward the target
- Support the victim by making a group or individual decision to show the bully that their behaviour is not acceptable
- Listen to the person being bullied and let them talk about how they are feeling

What you need to know about bullies

There are lots of different reasons people bully.

Some reasons identified by children include:

- Bullying makes them feel powerful and strong,
- It's a way to become known at school,
- They are scared themselves so try to scare others to hide their feelings and make themselves feel more in control,
- They are unhappy and take their negative feelings out on others,
- Often bullies come from homes where the parents use physical force to make their children behave. As a result, bullies have a lot of anger inside them.

Does bullying happen in the workplace? Yes, the same issues arise in adult environments too – which is another reason it is important for children to learn how to deal with bullying **NOW** so it doesn't become a life-long problem.

It may be hard understand but children who engage in bullying behaviours also have a right to be treated with respect. Research suggests that children who bully may have even higher levels of anxiety, stress, depression and self harm than their victims.

In the end, most bullies wind up in trouble. If they keep acting mean and hurtful, sooner or later they'll have only a few friends left - usually other children who are just like them.

The good news is that children who are bullies can learn to change their behaviour. Teachers, counsellors, and parents can help. Bullies can change and use their power in positive ways. Some bullies turn into great children.

So it's definitely worth the bully's parents and/or teachers helping bullies for two reasons:

Reason 1: No-one else will be victimised in their bullying game. There's always someone out there they can target so better to fix the bully!

Reason 2: So the bullies can lead a happy life themselves.

What is YOUR Primary Role in this

Imagine living in a world where everyone:

Do bullies respect themselves, everyone around them, their own and other people's property? Obviously not!

How about you? Do you respect yourself, everyone around you, your own and other people's property?

Respect

YOU, as a positive role model, are key to helping YOUR CHILD develop into a confident, caring, self-accepting individual.

References and Further Reading

Lopez, William. Successful Parenting Skills That Shape a Child's Behavior. N.p., 15 May 2004. Web. 20 May 2013.

Time for Tolerance. By children, for children http://library.thinkquest.org/07aug/00117/bullyingconsequences.html

http://www.empoweringparents.com/Is-Your-Child-Being-Bullied.php#

http://allpsych.com/journal/parentingskills.html

http://www.youthline.co.nz/services/69-information-andreferrals/1175-what-to-do-if-my-child-is-being-bullied.html

Telephone Help

Telephone help There are telephone help lines in all countries. Check on-line for those relevant to you and your child. For instance:

In UK:

http://familylives.org.uk/ Call 08088002222

http://www.youngminds.org.uk/for_parents/
parent_helpline Call 08088025544

In USA:

Just For Kids Hotline Call 1-888-594-KIDs

Girls and Boys Town National Hotline: Call
800-448-3000 or TDD: 800-448-1833

In Canada:

Kids Help Phone Call 1-800-668-6868

In New Zealand:

Kidsline Call 0800 KIDSLINE (New Zealand 0800 543 754)

What's Up Telephone counselling for 5-18
year olds. Call (0800) 942 8787

Youthline Call (0800) 37 66 33 or email talk@youthline.co.nz

In Australia:

http://www.kidshelp.com.au/teens/ Call 1800551800

http://www.youthbeyondblue.com/get-help/
phone-help-lines/ Call 1300 22 4636

Appendix I – Role-play Guidance

Role-play. You will want to identify what the desired behaviour looks like. Tell your child that first you will play him and he will pretend he is you. Make it fun. Run through a scenario leading up to a bullying moment, then try some different responses. Then give your child a chance to practice the preferred option, playing himself, several times.

Talk about it. Discuss when and where you think he would get to try out this new set of behaviour in real life.

Reference back. Once the child has tried it out in 'real life' (successfully or unsuccessfully), discuss what happened. e.g. 'What did you do?' 'How did that feel?' 'Did the role play we practiced help?' 'What will you do next time?'

If it doesn't work. Your child may not develop this new skill right away. Remember, he/she has been in the habit of doing it differently. He/she is going to need many new experiences of the behaviour done correctly in order for change to occur. Keep at it!

Be very positive and supporting of any progress he has made no matter how small. You want to encourage the positive replacement behaviour as much as possible.

Lightning Source UK Ltd.
Milton Keynes UK
UKHW021435280322
400723UK00007B/1395

9 780473 249847